The Little Follow the Dots Book

Anna Pomaska

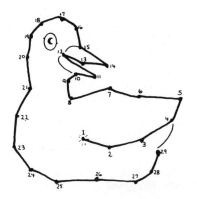

Dover Publications, New York

by Nathan

Shock.

Published in Canada by General Publishing Company, Ltd.,
30 Lesmill Road, Don Mills, Toronto, Ontario.
Published in the United Kingdom by Constable and Company, Ltd.

The Little Follow the Dots Book is a new work, first published by Dover Publications, Inc., in 1986.

International Standard Book Number: 0-486-25157-8

Manufactured in the United States of America
Dover Publications, Inc., 31 East 2nd Street,
Mineola, N.Y. 11501

Publisher's Note

This book is full of dots and full of fun! You'll enjoy linking the dots together to create 58 delightful pictures. The fun, though, begins even before you start connecting the dots. As you come to each puzzle, first read the short rhyme at the bottom of the page and see if you can guess what picture the connected dots will form. Then, using a pencil or pen, draw a line from dot number 1 to dot number 2, and then from dot number 2 to dot number 3, 3 to 4, 4 to 5, and so on. Continue on in this manner until you have connected all the numbered dots. Was your guess correct? If perhaps you made a mistake along the way—one of the puzzles has over 90 dots!—and you're not sure what the picture is of, you can check the list of pictures at the back of the book. Of course, when you've finished following the dots, you then get to color the pictures. You'll see pictures of all sorts of animals, things that are out of this world and many other familiar objects. Now, if you are ready, it's time for the fun to begin: Follow those dots!

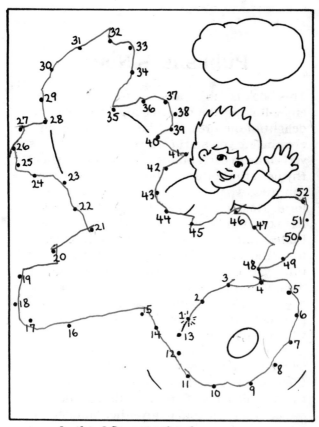

In this I fly up in the sky,
Watching the clouds float gently by.

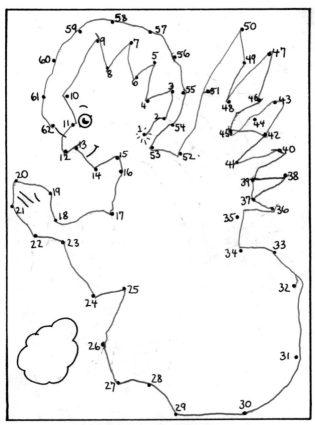

Here is someone full of joy
Who loves every girl and boy.

5

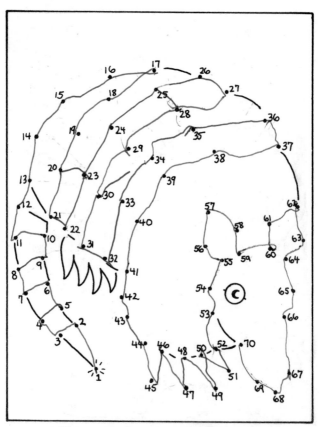

This animal wears a coat of armor
So that it's difficult to harm her.

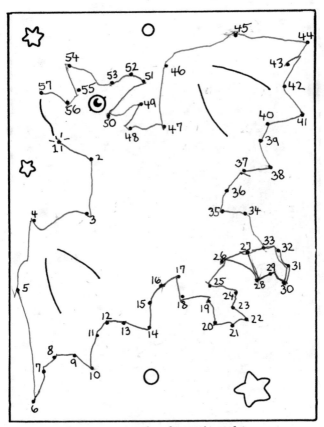

I come out only when it's night,
And fly away when it turns light.

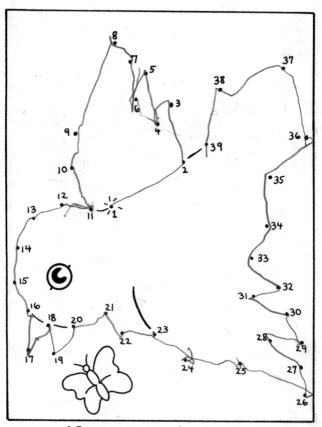

I flap my wings and up I go;
Then I can see the things below.

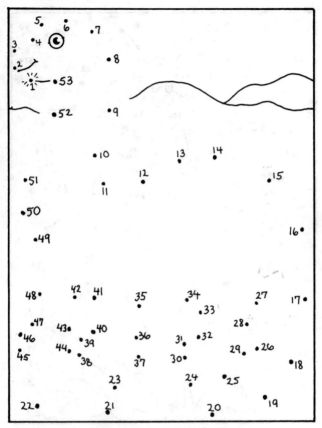

As dinosaurs go, this creature is famous.
Do you happen to know what its long name is?

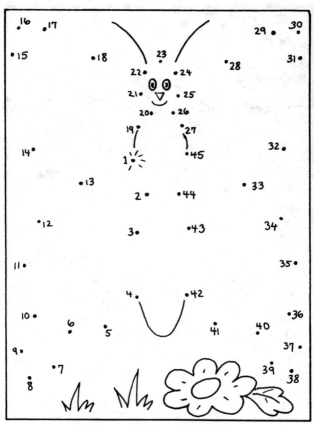

In the sunny meadow I play
And visit the flowers all day.

If you like to go down the street,
Traveling in this is quite a treat.

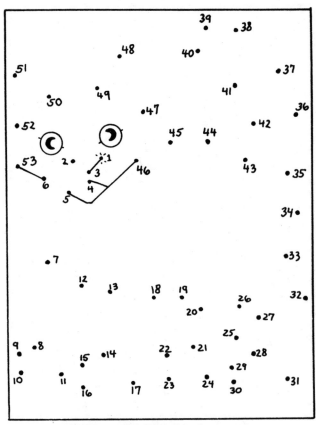

Here is a pet that's black as night.
Can you bring him into sight?

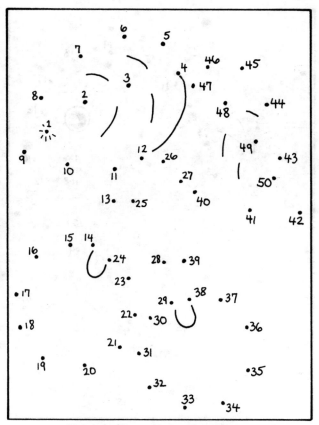

If you look up at a certain tree,
Here's the fruit that you will see.

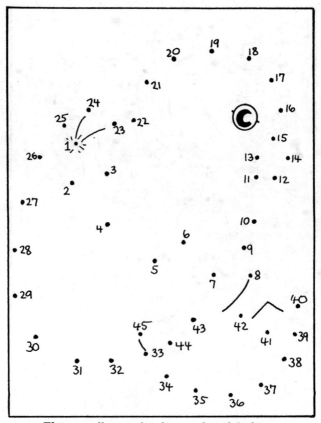

This small, cute bird is such a delight.
You'll find it has just now hatched into sight.

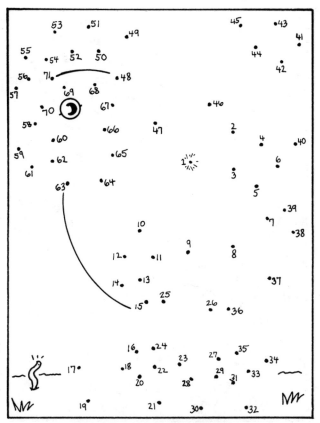

I am always looking around
For food to peck off the ground.

15

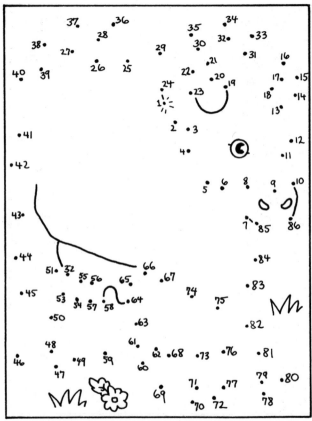

I like to graze in a meadow all day,
Or stand in a barn and chew my hay.

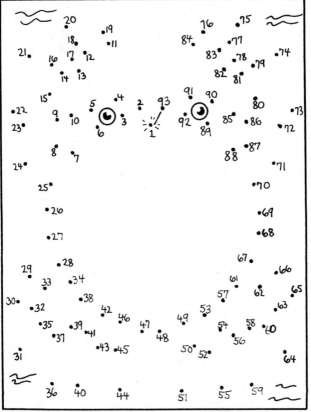

I'm a creature you'll find in the sea.
Can you guess what animal I might be?

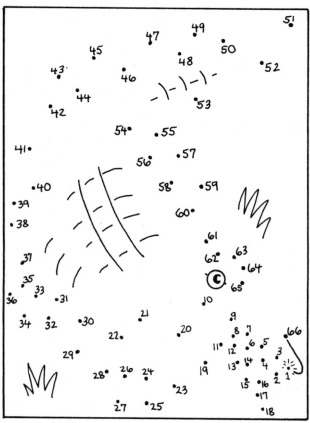

This animal just loves to romp
In a very wet and murky swamp.

I love to spend all day with you.
I'm your best friend and you're mine, too.

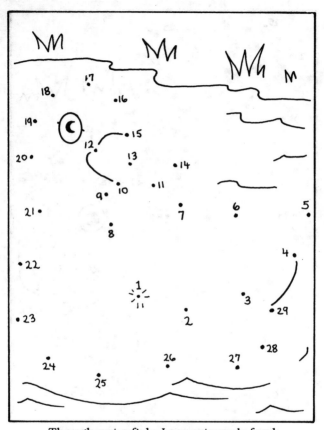

Though not a fish, I am extremely fond
Of swimming in the little pond.

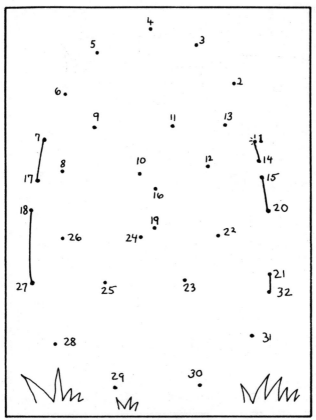

This is a very special thing.
A bunny brings it every spring.

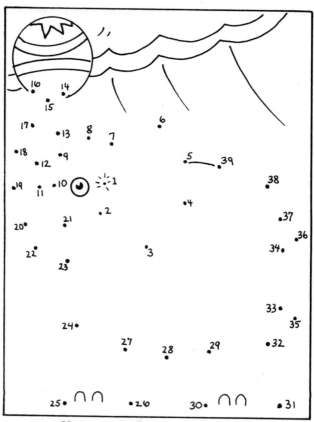

Here is a performer with his ball.
Can you tell if he's big or small?

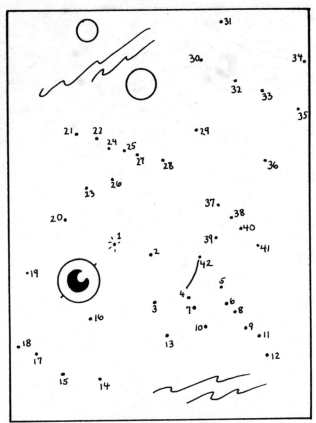

In the water, to and fro,
Swimming all the day I go.

23

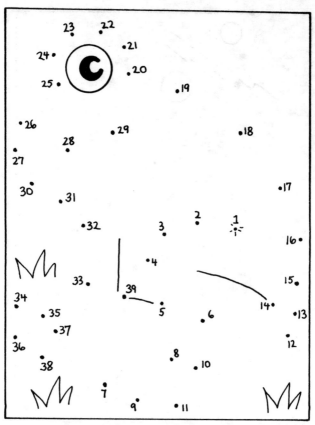

At a pond you may have seen
This tailless leaper colored green.

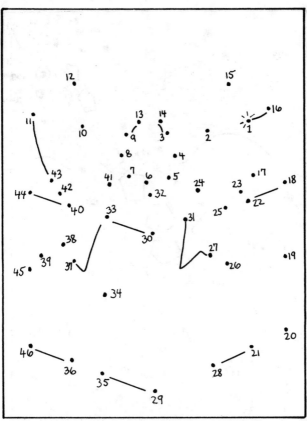

When you give someone one of these,
You usually hope to please.

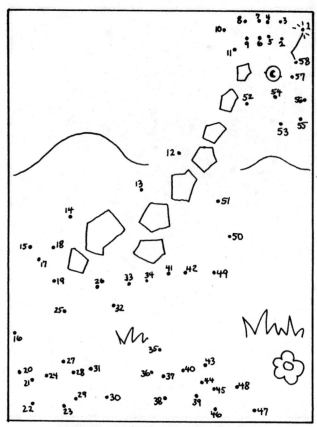

I must admit I'm not very small;
The fact is I'm actually quite tall.

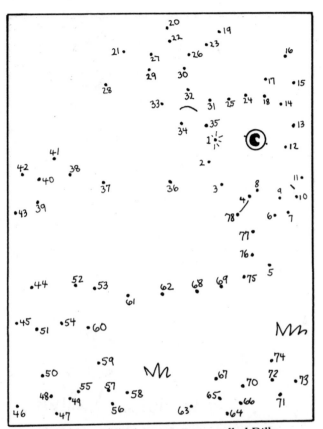

Here is an animal sometimes called Billy.
Don't get too close or he'll butt you silly.

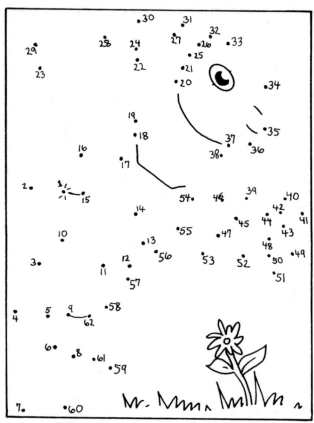

When you see this insect jump so high,
You might think he will reach the sky.

This is something you might try
When looking for a way to fly.

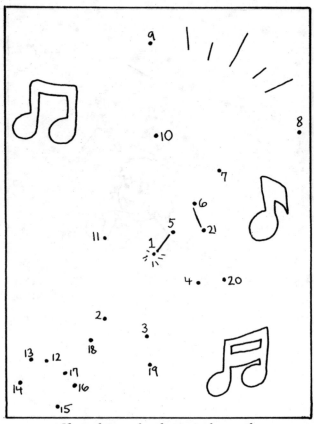

If you hear a loud musical sound,
You will know that I'm around.

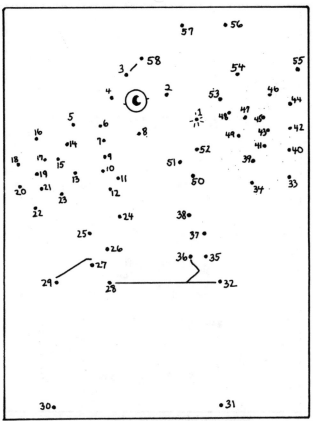

You may want to jump with fright
When this fellow comes in sight.

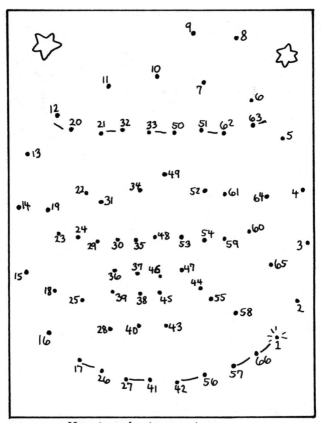

Here is a glowing mystery.
What can this scary creature be?

Over and under rocks I crawl,
And also run along the wall.

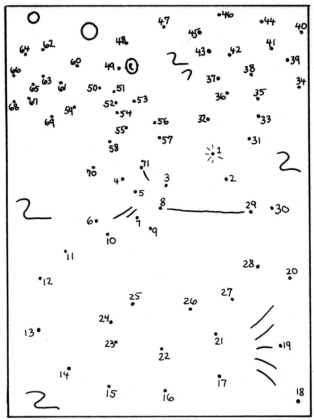

I look almost like you, but I live in the water,
34 And I'm sometimes known as Neptune's daughter.

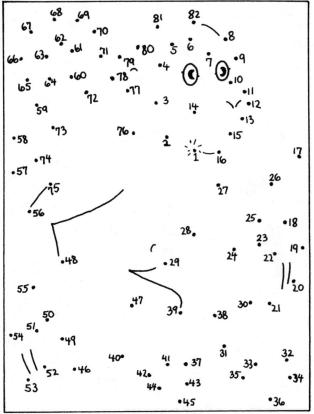

When you see this fellow, don't you run,
For if you do, you'll miss the fun.

35

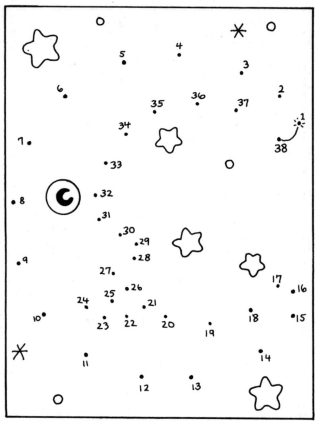

Can you guess whose smiling face
You will find out here in space?

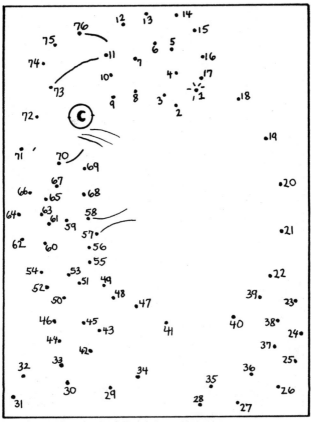

This little fellow's most at ease
When he's chomping on his cheese.

You never need to stray or roam;
There's plenty of "room" inside my home.

38

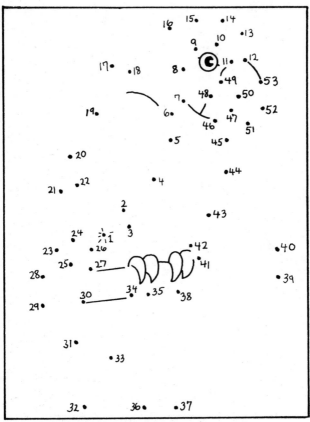

Here's a bird that loves to squawk
Almost as much as he loves to talk.

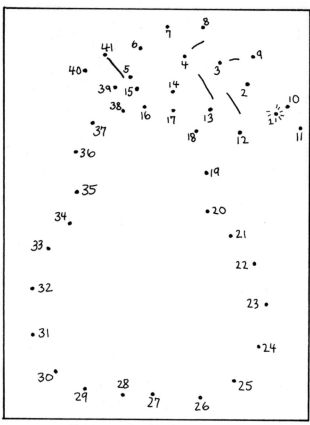

If you want a fruity treat,
Here is something good to eat.

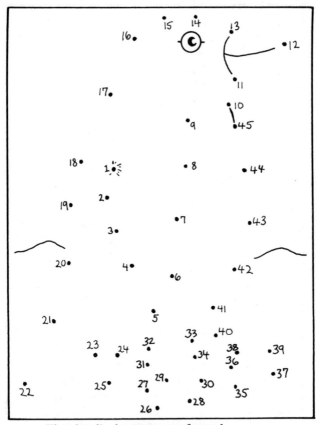

This bird's dress is very formal.
He thinks that snow and ice are normal.   41

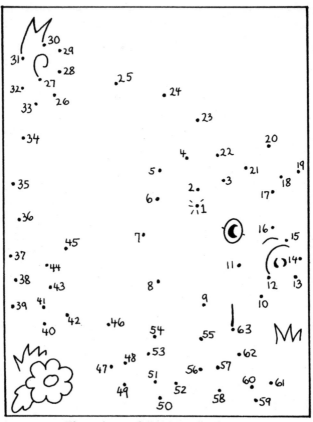

This plump fellow can be found
Eating everything around.

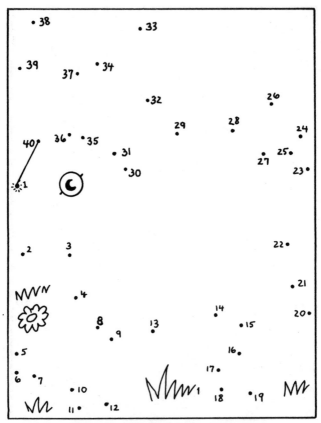

This is someone who will bring
A special present in the spring.

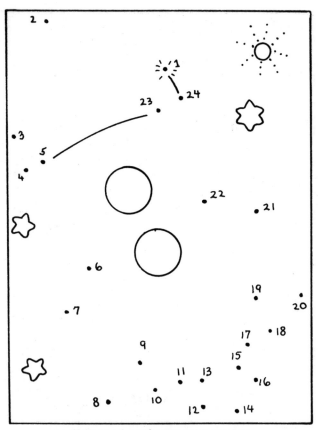

Here is something out in space,
Traveling to a far-off place.

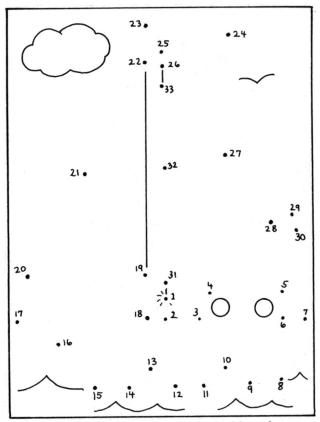

If not for the wind this craft would not be
Able to travel over the sea.

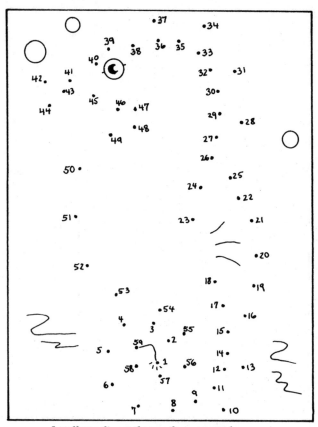

I gallop along through every tide,
Looking for sea folks who want a ride.

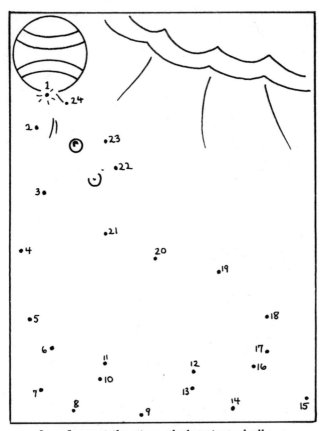

I perform at the circus balancing a ball.
I hope I don't sneeze, for then it would fall.

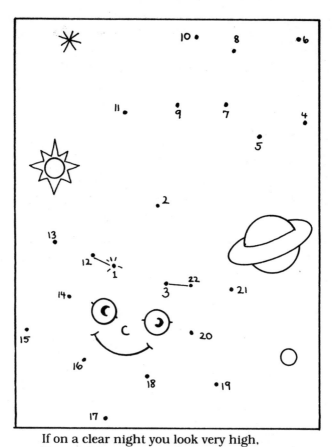

If on a clear night you look very high,
You might see me streaking across the dark sky.

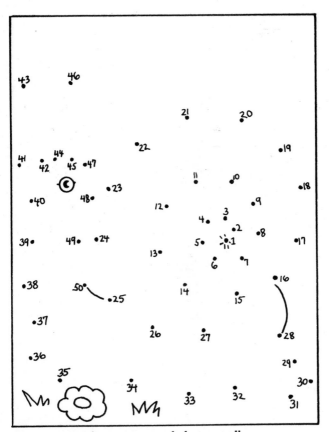

Here is something you surely know well:
This creature moves slowly and carries its shell.   49

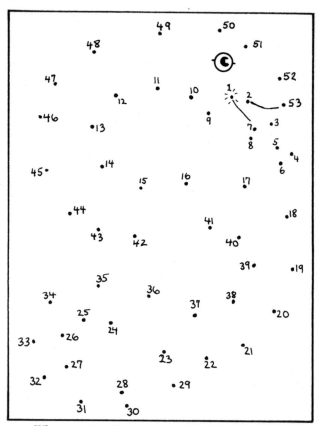

When out in the woods and looking around,
You might see me slither by on the ground.

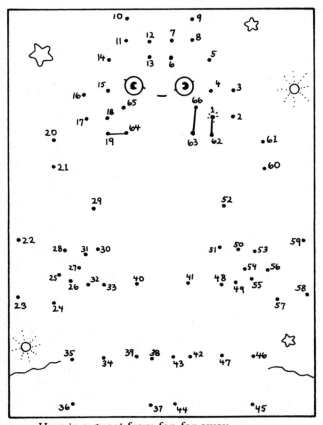

Here is a guest from far, far away.
He has traveled to Earth to join you at play. 51

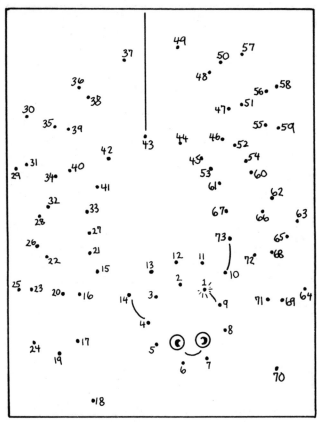

Whenever this fellow drops into sight,
He often gives us quite a fright.

52

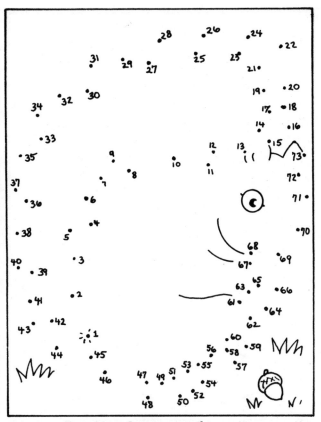

Every year I run around,
Gathering acorns on the ground.

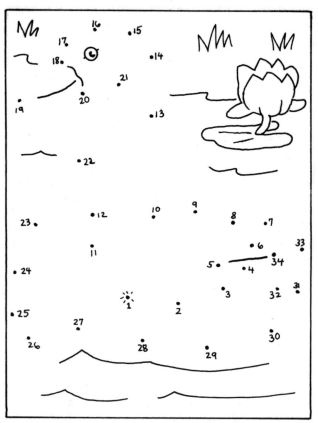

A graceful swimmer, white as a cloud,
My fine long neck makes me most proud.

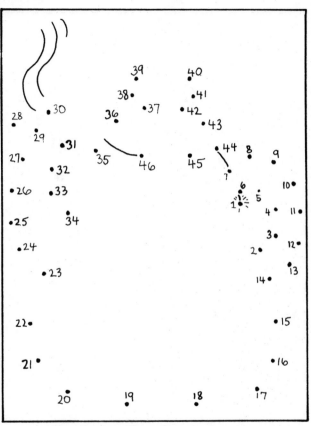

I have a handle and a spout,
And hold the tea that you pour out.

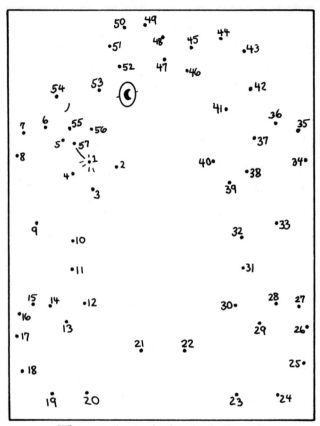

When you're tucked in bed all snug,
You will find me there to hug.

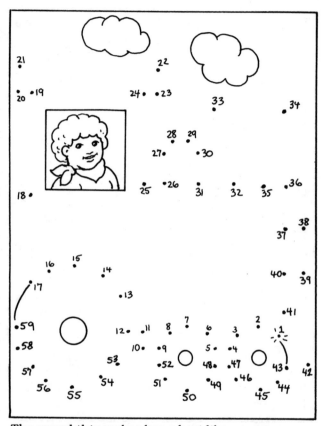

The sound this makes has a beat like a song,
When down the track it comes chugging along. 57

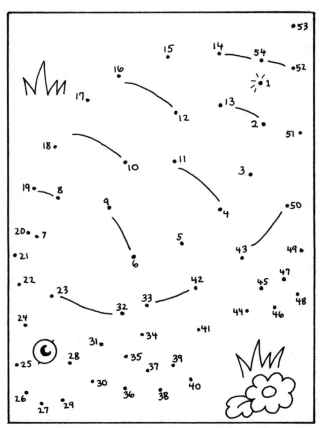

Here's a reptile you're sure to know.
He's very famous for being slow.

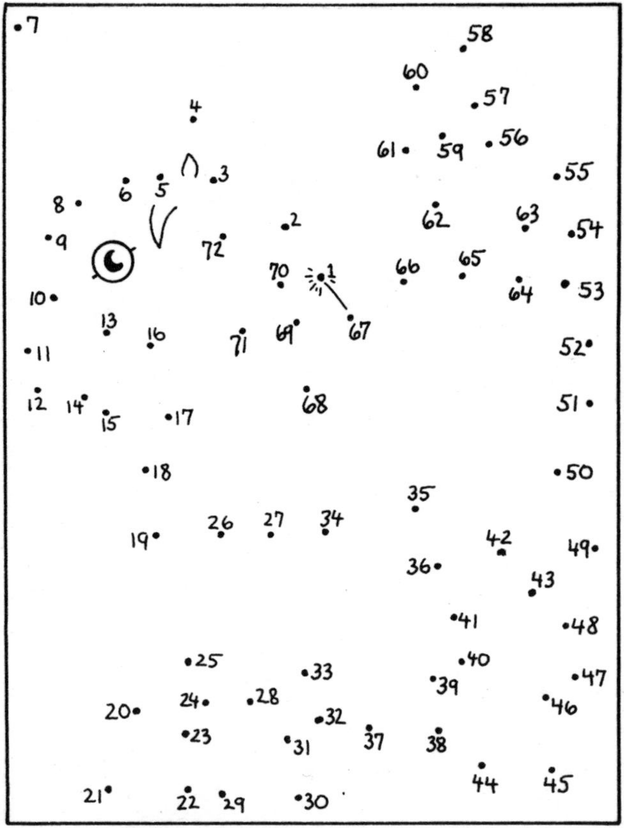

•7

•58

•60

•57

•4

61• 59• •56

8• •6 •5 ∩ •3

•55

•8 •62 •63 •54

•9 •2

•72 •70 •1 •66 •65 •64 •53

•10 •13 •71 69• •67

•16 52•

•11

•12 •14 •68 51•

•15 •17

•18 •50

•35

•19 •26 •27 •34 •42 •49

•36 •43

•41 •48

•25 •40 •47

•33 •39 •46

20• 24• •28

•23 •32 •37 •38 •44 •45

•31

21• 22 •29 •30

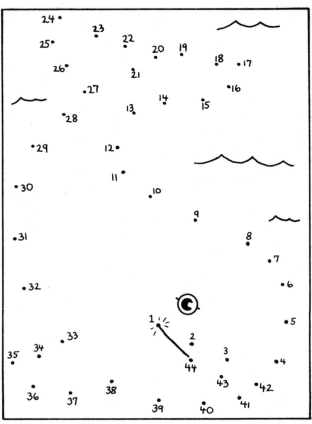

I'm a beast you'll recognize,
If only for my giant size.

On Halloween night, if you're out and about,
You'll see me fly by, and you'll give such a shout!

Identifying the Pictures

Connect the dots, 1, 2 and 3, . . . ,
And this is the picture you will see.